CHILDREN LIKE US
Food
AROUND THE WORLD

Moira Butterfield

Cavendish
Square

New York

Published in 2016 by Cavendish Square Publishing, LLC
243 5th Avenue, Suite 136, New York, NY 10016

First Edition

Website: cavendishsq.com

This publication represents the opinions and views of the author based on his or her personal experience, knowledge, and research. The information in this book serves as a general guide only. The author and publisher have used their best efforts in preparing this book and disclaim liability rising directly or indirectly from the use and application of this book.

CPSIA Compliance Information: Batch #WW16CSQ

All websites were available and accurate when this book was sent to press.However, it is possible that contents or addresses may have changed since the publication of this book. No responsibility for any such changes can be accepted by either the author or the Publisher.

Cataloging-in-Publication Data

Butterfield, Moira.
Food around the world / by Moira Butterfield.
p. cm. — (Children like us)
Includes index.
ISBN 978-1-5026-0840-6 (hardcover) ISBN 978-1-5026-0838-3 (paperback) ISBN 978-1-5026-0841-3 (ebook)
1. Food habits — Juvenile literature. 2. Food — Juvenile literature. I. Butterfield, Moira, 1960-. II. Title.
TX355.B88 2016
641.3—d23

Editor: Izzi Howell
Designer: Clare Nicholas
Picture researcher: Izzi Howell
Proofreaders: Izzi Howell/Stephen White-Thomson
Wayland editor: Annabel Stones

Picture credits:
The author and publisher would like to thank the following for allowing their pictures to be reproduced in this publication: cover Anna Issakova/Shutterstock.com; p.3 (t-b) mkistryn/iStock, Perfect Lazybones/Shutterstock, Nataliya Arzamasova/Shutterstock, Sarah Bossert/iStock; pp.4-5 (c) ekler/Shutterstock, p.4 (t) bhofack2/iStock, (b) enviromantic/iStock; p.5 (tl) bonchan/iStock, (tr) szefei/Shutterstock, (b) idome/Shutterstock; p.6 (t) xuanhuongho/Shutterstock, (b) bonchan/iStock; p.7 (l) Amanda Koster/Corbis, (r) Lauri Patterson/iStock; p.8 (t) szefei/Shutterstock, (bl) Nataliya Arzamasova/Shutterstock, (br) HLPhoto/Shutterstock; p.9 Ron Nickel/Design Pics/Corbis; p.10 (tl) Africa Studio/Shutterstock, (tr) Tatyana Gladskikh/Dreamstime, (b) Staffan Widstrand/Corbis; p.11 (l) Gil Giuglio/Hemis/Corbis, (r) picturepartners/Shutterstock; p.12 (t) Hasse Bengtsson/Johnér Images/Corbis, (b) Krzysztof Slusarczyk/Shutterstock, p.13 (t) lsantilli/Shutterstock, (b) bhofack2/iStock; p.14 (t) Oleg Baliuk/Shutterstock, (b) Li Luan Han / Redlink/Redlink/Corbis; p.15 IndiaImages/iStock; p.16 (tl) Chen Li/Xinhua Press/Corbis, (tr) fotohunter/Shutterstock, (b) pamspix/iStock; p.17 neelsky/Shutterstock; p.18 (t) eurobanks/iStock, (b) Bartosz Hadyniak/iStock; p.19 (t) Bartosz Hadyniak/iStock, (b) Stringer/India/Reuters/Corbis; p.20 (t) Tomophafan/Shutterstock, (bl) enviromantic/iStock, (br) mkistryn/iStock; p.21 javarman/Shutterstock; p.22 Yadid Levy/Robert Harding World Imagery/Corbis; p.23 (tr) JMWScout/iStock, (c) Sarah Bossert/iStock, (bl) xuanhuongho/iStock; p.24 (tl) Bartosz Hadyniak/iStock, (cr) Sarah Bossert/iStock, (br) Elena Mirage/Shutterstock; p.26 (t) astudio/Shutterstock, (b) Orietta Gaspari/Shutterstock; p.27 (t) Peathegee Inc/Blend Images/Corbis, (b) Perfect Lazybones/Shutterstock; pp.28-29 Remi Benali/Corbis; p.29 (l) idome/Shutterstock, (r) Perfect Lazybones/Shutterstock; p.30 (l-r, t-b) neelsky/Shutterstock, enviromantic/iStock, vertmedia/iStock, Nataliya Arzamasova/Shutterstock, bonchan/iStock, eurobanks/iStock, idome/Shutterstock, lsantilli/Shutterstock, mipstudio/Shutterstock, mkistryn/iStock, Africa Studio/Shutterstock, fotohunter/Shutterstock, Tatyana Gladskikh/Dreamstime, HLPhoto/Shutterstock; p.31 (l) javarman/Shutterstock, (r) IndiaImages/iStock.

Design elements used throughout: Oksancia/Shutterstock, lilac/Shutterstock, Dacian G/Shutterstock, rassco/Shutterstock, Aliaksei_7799/Shutterstock, Jane Rix/Shutterstock, id-work/iStock, pandora64/Shutterstock, AKIllustration/Shutterstock, PinkPueblo/Shutterstock, ksana-gribakina/Shutterstock, Turkan Akyol/Shutterstock, kasahasa/Shutterstock, oxygendesign021/Shutterstock, akiradesigns/Shutterstock, tsirik/Shutterstock, Anton Lunkov/Shutterstock, rustamank/Shutterstock, LSF421/Shutterstock, Macrovector/Shutterstock.

Printed in the United States of America

Contents

All Kinds of Food

Are you ready to find out about the food eaten by children around the world? You'll learn what people eat at meal times. Plus, you'll find out what they eat and drink on special days. There's a whole world to discover!

What foods can you see at this American Thanksgiving meal? Find out on page 13.

Different fruits grow in each country. Learn the name of this one on page 20.

Some people start the day with sweet foods. Find out about this treat on page 6.

Discover the story behind this Indian lunch dish on page 8.

Can you picture eating a Cambodian fried tarantula? Find out more on page 29.

Take a trip around the world to learn about food eaten by children just like you!

What's for Breakfast?

This lady is serving up a Vietnamese bowl of breakfast. It is a noodle soup called pho. It's a spicy broth made with chicken or beef and rice noodles.

It takes many hours to boil up a good pho broth.

Does chocolate for breakfast sound good? Make sure you try churros from Spain. They are often served with a chocolate sauce for dipping.

Churros can be dipped in hot chocolate or milky coffee.

This is a Mexican breakfast dish. A tortilla is topped with tomatoes, beans, rice, and eggs.

This Guatemalan girl holds a bowl of corn paste. It will be flattened and cooked to make tortillas.

In Central America, corn tortillas are often eaten at breakfast. Tortillas can be used in lots of ways. They can be wrapped around meat or eggs. They can be cut into strips and fried. They can be baked, too.

What's for Lunch?

These little piles of spicy Indian food are called *chaat*. The story goes that a doctor invented *chaat*. It was used to cure an Indian emperor called Sha Jahan. In India, spices are thought to be healthy medicine.

This chaat lunch rests on a banana leaf.

Here is a *kawaii* bento box. The food makes a picture of two cute pandas.

In Japan, children often take bento boxes to school for lunch. Bento boxes contain small amounts of different foods. Making *kawaii* bento boxes is popular in Japan. In this kind of box, the food is made into pictures. "Kawaii" means "cute" in Japanese.

A normal bento box might contain sushi. Sushi is a roll with raw fish.

This girl from Mozambique in Africa is having a common African lunch. She is eating rice and beans that have been made into a spicy stew.

Different kinds of rice and bean dishes are served all over Africa.

What's for Dinner?

Have you had pasta for dinner? Pasta was first made in Italy almost one thousand years ago. At that time, they used lettuce juice to give the pasta a green color. Pasta is now the most popular food in the world!

There are around five hundred different kinds of pasta, each with its own Italian name.

This girl is having "little strings" for dinner. That's what "spaghetti" means!

In the icy far north of Canada, there aren't many shops or restaurants. People hunt for their dinner. This Nunavut boy is catching arctic char through a hole in the ice.

The Arctic Ocean is covered with ice for most of the year. The Nunavut cut holes in the ice to fish.

This Tunisian boy is buying spices in an outdoor market. These spices will be used to flavor his dinner of *koksi*. *Koksi* is couscous served with spicy meat and vegetables.

This is *koksi*, which is commonly eaten in Tunisia in Africa.

Harissa is a common Tunisian spice. It is a spicy paste made of roasted peppers and dried spices.

Festival Food

Food is important at festivals. In Sweden, they celebrate St. Lucia's Day on December 13. That morning, the oldest girl in a family gives her parents a plate of special buns for breakfast.

This girl is helping to bake buns, called *lussekat*, for St. Lucia's Day.

Some people think the Swedish buns look like cats. In fact, *lussekat* means "Lucia's cats."

A special meal is served on New Year's Eve in Italy. The dish has lentils to symbolize good fortune. It has pork, too. The meat stands for the richness of life. Everybody eats some of the dish for good luck in the coming year!

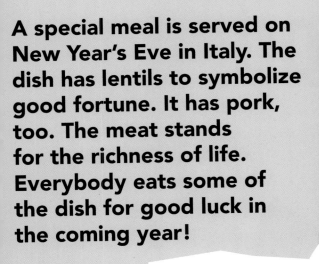

The sausage slices are coin-shaped. As they eat, people hope their lives will be filled with plenty.

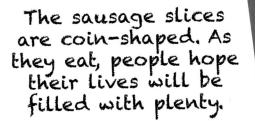

People in the USA celebrate Thanksgiving. It celebrates an earlier meal. In 1620, the Native American people helped the first European settlers live through a harsh winter. To say thank you, they shared a big meal together.

On Thanksgiving, foods such as turkey and cranberries are eaten to celebrate American history.

Wedding Food

The tradition of eating a wedding cake started around two thousand years ago. At the end of an Ancient Roman wedding, the groom broke a small cake over the bride's head. The guests ate the crumbs to share the couple's good fortune.

Today, the bride and groom cut the wedding cake. Then they share it with their guests.

This Chinese bride gives out sweets to her guests. Chinese wedding sweets are often made from peanuts and sugar. They are coated with crunchy sesame seeds, too.

These Chinese wedding guests eat a feast of many different dishes.

These Indian women are at a four-day wedding feast.

Everyone has special meals for the guests at a wedding. In India, it's more than just one meal. It's a four-day feast! At the end, any leftover food gets shared with the local village.

Sweet Treats

During the Chinese Moon Festival, it's traditional to eat moon cakes. These are filled with bean paste and egg yolks. The cakes have Chinese characters on top. It is said they were once used to pass secret messages between Chinese rebels.

The Chinese characters on moon cakes say things like "long life."

Moon cakes were first eaten to honor a Chinese moon goddess.

Anzac cookies are made with oats, coconut, and syrup.

On April 25, sweet, buttery Anzac cookies are eaten in Australia and New Zealand. They are made for Anzac Day. On this day, people remember the soldiers who fought in World Wars I and II. Anzac cookies were sent to soldiers fighting overseas.

This Indian boy is enjoying a snack of raw sugarcane. You can't eat the hard outer part of the cane, but when you chew the soft inner core, sugary juice comes out.

This sugarcane will keep this Indian boy busy for a long time.

Delicious Drinks

Bubble tea tastes like a sweet milky smoothie, with added chewy bits.

Have you tried bubble tea yet? It was invented in Taiwan in the 1980s. Now the craze has spread to other countries. There are many different flavors to try. Plus, there are chewy tapioca or jelly balls at the bottom.

This Tibetan monk is making butter tea.

If you visited somebody in Tibet, you would be offered butter tea. It is made from tea leaves mixed with yak butter, salt, and water. Your host will keep filling up your cup until you leave.

Moroccan mint tea is poured from a height. This makes it taste better.

These Sri Lankan girls are enjoying a drink of coconut water. You only need to drill or cut a hole into a coconut and add a straw for an instant drink!

You can only drink coconut water from young coconuts without a hard outer shell.

Fantastic Fruit

This is the world's smelliest fruit! It's called a durian. It grows in Malaysia. It is said to smell like rotting onions mixed with sweaty socks. Its soft flesh tastes like ripe banana, though.

The durian fruit smells so badly that it has been banned on trains in Singapore.

This yellow fruit is a Buddha's Hand from India. It tastes like a lemon. The pretty pink fruit is a pitahaya, or dragon fruit. It grows in Mexico and Central America. It tastes similar to watermelon.

Pitahayas grow on spiky cactus plants.

This lady is selling fruit in a market in Colombia. Her basket of tropical fruits includes pineapple and melon. People in Europe had never seen or tasted these fruits until they explored the Americas in 1492.

Tropical fruits were once only enjoyed by people who lived in tropical places. Now they are shipped around the world.

The Buddha's Hand is sometimes kept in a room to make the air smell like lemon.

All Kinds of Vegetables

Seaweed is grown on ropes between sticks under water.

This African teenager lives in Zanzibar in Tanzania. She is harvesting seaweed. It will be sold to China and Japan. There, it will be eaten as a vegetable.

This person is cutting up nopales. These are the pads of a prickly pear cactus with the spikes removed. Nopales are popular in Mexico. The round vegetables below are the tips of fern plants. They are called fiddleheads. They are eaten in the United States.

Fiddleheads are harvested in the spring.

Nopales are fried or used in salads.

In this Vietnamese market, you can buy different kinds of root vegetables. They sell taro, manioc, and sweet potatoes. In tropical places, people cook these vegetables like potatoes. They also grind them up to make flour.

The largest root vegetables here are called manioc. Manioc is used to make tapioca. That's what the bubbles in bubble tea are made from (see page 18).

Yummy Bread

Bread is eaten all around the world. There are lots of different kinds of bread. Across Asia and Africa, flatbread is really popular. People bake flatbreads on open fires and sell them at roadside stalls.

In Ethiopia, a flatbread called injera is used instead of a plate! People rip off small pieces of the injera to scoop up the food.

Flatbreads are round and flat, like pancakes.

Sometimes bread has its own story. These round loaves are called *tokoch*. They are made in Kyrgyzstan in Asia. It is said that if you want good luck, you should bake seven *tokoch* loaves, then give them to seven different people.

In Kyrgyzstan, you might be offered a piece of *tokoch* with some plum jam.

These Turkish *simit* loaves are being sold fresh from the oven.

This Turkish boy is selling delicious *simit*. It is a round loaf covered in crunchy sesame seeds. He carries the loaves on his head. *Simit* has been sold like this for many centuries in Turkey and Greece.

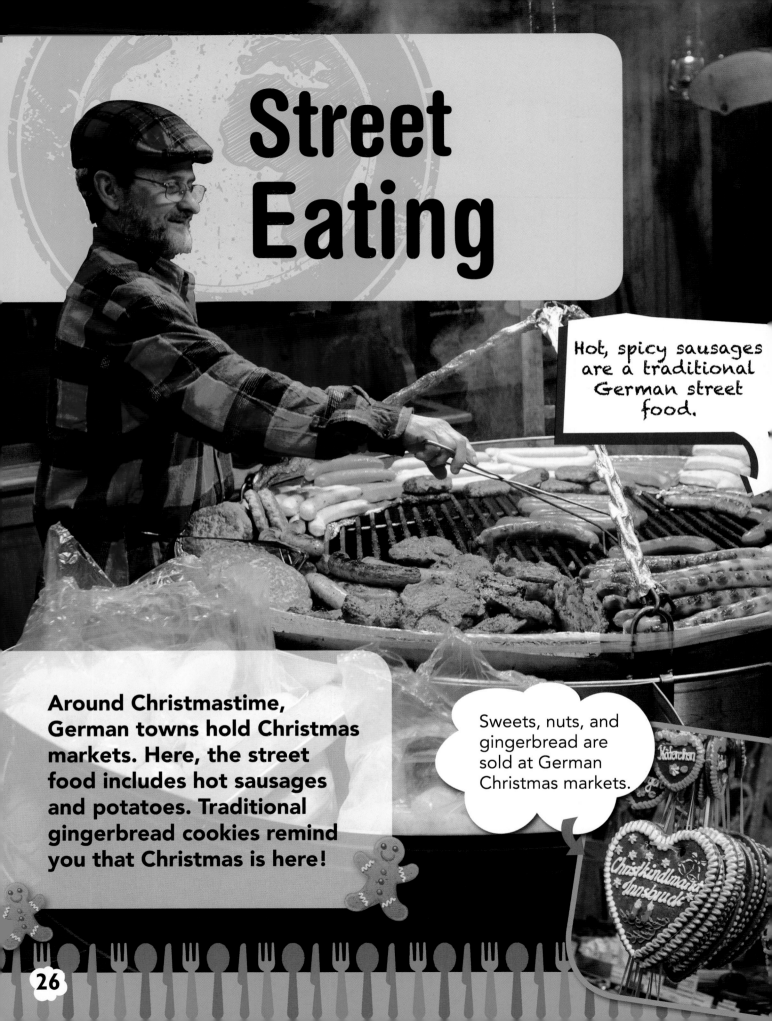

Street Eating

Hot, spicy sausages are a traditional German street food.

Around Christmastime, German towns hold Christmas markets. Here, the street food includes hot sausages and potatoes. Traditional gingerbread cookies remind you that Christmas is here!

Sweets, nuts, and gingerbread are sold at German Christmas markets.

These children are enjoying snow cones from a food truck in Los Angeles, USA. Food trucks are vans fitted with kitchens so that food can be prepared on board. Food trucks park on streets sell all kinds of food.

Snow cones are a popular treat in America. Flavored syrup is poured over crushed ice.

This woman is selling street food in Cambodia, a country in southeast Asia. Her basket is filled with *num kom*. These are steamed banana leaf packages filled with rice dough and sweet coconut. She probably makes the food herself every day and sells it to make a living.

The word "num" means "cake" in Khmer, a language spoken in Cambodia.

Now THAT'S Different!

This Sumatran boy is eating ants straight from the nest. They taste sweet, like honey. Insects are cooked and eaten in many African and Asian countries. They are full of protein, which is important in a balanced diet.

Ants can be fried, toasted, or even made into cakes.

The crunchy-looking food below is fried grasshoppers sold in a Thai food market. You could also go to Cambodia to eat a fried tarantula spider. They taste nutty. Head to China to eat baby bees that taste like mushrooms. Maybe you'd rather go to Mexico to eat fried agave worms? They taste like sunflower seeds!

These fried grasshoppers taste fishy.

Fried tarantulas are usually the size of the palm of your hand.

Art Station

Here are some ideas to help you get creative and become an amazing chef!

- What is your favorite breakfast dish? Draw a picture of it and label the ingredients.

- Create a new dish using fruit. Draw a picture of it, give it a name, and label the ingredients.

- Design a stall to sell street food. Work out what kind of food you're going to sell and give your stall a name.

- Design a cake for a party. It could be a wedding cake, a birthday cake, or a cake for some other special occasion.

Glossary

bento box A Japanese lunch box.

broth Another word for soup.

dough Flour mixed with water.

edible Something you can eat.

festival A day or a period of a few days when everyone celebrates something.

flatbread Bread that does not have yeast in it to make it rise.

ingredients Types of food put together to make a recipe.

noodles Long thin strips made from different types of flour mixed with water.

pasta Strips or little shapes made from wheat flour mixed with water.

protein A part of food that helps your body to grow strong and stay healthy.

root vegetable The edible root of a plant.

spice Flavoring made from parts of a dried plant, such as seeds, roots or bark.

symbol Something that represents an idea.

tradition Something that has been going on for a long time.

tropical Hot weather found in parts of the world around the Equator, an imaginary line around the middle of the earth.

Further Information

Websites

Around the World - TIME for Kids
This website offers a closer look at world cultures, including the foods unique to them.
www.timeforkids.com/around-the-world

Chinese Food for Kids
A website dedicated to teaching kids about traditional Chinese foods.
www.china-family-adventure.com/chinese-food.html

Kids Cooking Activities
A guide to foods around the world, including recipes and language tips.
www.kids-cooking-activities.com/international-gourmet-recipes.html

Books

D'Aluisio, Faith and Peter Menzel. *What the World Eats*. New York: Random House, 2008.

DK. *A Life Like Mine: How Children Live Around the World*. New York: DK Children, 2005.

Shea, Mary Molly. *Foods of India*. New York: Gareth Stevens Publishing, 2011.

Sheen, Barbara. *Foods of Colombia*. San Diego, CA: KidHaven Press, 2012.

Index